AF432333

Quizzical

800+ Questions to Fuel Creativity and Curiosity

Hey!

This book is a creative resource.

Read it.

Write in it.

Share it with loved ones.

-Deja

Deja Cherese
Quizzical: 800+ Questions to Fuel Creativity and Curiosity
© 2020, Deja Cherese
Self-published

Table of Contents

How to Use This Book..............................1

Chapter 1: Self Expression......................3

    Quiz 1 – The Look
    Quiz 2 – Interior Design
    Quiz 3 – Doodles, Voice, and Songs
    Quiz 4 – Influences

Chapter 2: Creativity..............................11

    Quiz 1 – Experience and Opinion
    Quiz 2 – The Arts
    Quiz 3 – Creative Process
    Quiz 4 – Inventions
    Quiz 5 – Creative Problem Solving
    Quiz 6 – Creative Hybrids

Chapter 3: Finances...............................19

    Quiz 1 – Financial Finesse
    Quiz 2 – Rich Mom
    Quiz 3 – Poor Mom
    Quiz 4 – Hustle and Jive
    Quiz 5 – The Art of Money
    Quiz 6 – Financial Goals

Chapter 4: Food, Drinks and Sleep.........27

    Quiz 1 – Foodies
    Quiz 2 – Ice Cold Drinks
    Quiz 3 – Sleep Preferences
    Quiz 4   Wild Things

Quiz 5 – Kitchen & Cooking Habits
Quiz 6 – Sleep Habits

Chapter 5: Community and Society.......35

Quiz 1 – Fears and Hopes
Quiz 2 – Politics
Quiz 3 – Economics
Quiz 4 – Education
Quiz 5 – Environment

Chapter 6: Jobs, Careers and Purpose...43

Quiz 1 – Dream Jobs
Quiz 2 – Job Stereotypes
Quiz 3 – Overall Opinion
Quiz 4 – Work Readiness
Quiz 5 – Customer Service
Quiz 6 – Vacations

Chapter 7: The Present of the Past........53

Quiz 1 – 10 Years Ago
Quiz 2 – School Memories and Field Trips
Quiz 3 – Old Appearances, Looks, Fashion
Quiz 4 – People Who Hurt, Heal, and Humor
Quiz 5 – Parenting and Elder Care
Quiz 6 – Home Remedies and Cures

Chapter 8: The Future............................65

Quiz 1 – Predictions
Quiz 2 – Personal Goals
Quiz 3 – Technology
Quiz 4 – Time Travel and Superpowers
Quiz 5 – What Needs to Come Back?
Quiz 6 – Outer Space

Chapter 9: Pop Culture...........................73

Quiz 1 – Music

Quiz 2 – Movies/TV
Quiz 3 – Games
Quiz 4 – Fashion
Quiz 5 – Stars
Quiz 6 – Dances, Festivals, and Outings

Chapter 10: Milestones..............................83

Quiz 1 – Marriage
Quiz 2 – Birthdays
Quiz 3 – Driving
Quiz 4 – Holidays
Quiz 5 – Transportation
Quiz 6 – Health Consciousness

Chapter 11: Spirituality.............................91

Quiz 1 – Religious Upbringing
Quiz 2 – Current Beliefs
Quiz 3 – Best Life Experiences
Quiz 4 – Life Rituals
Quiz 5 – Personal Maintenance and Rejuvenation
Quiz 6 – Health Consciousness

Chapter 12: Biopic.....................................101

Quiz 1 – Life Stats
Quiz 2 – Family History
Quiz 3 – Hobbies
Quiz 4 – Comfort Zone Definers
Quiz 5 – Socializing Styles
Quiz 6 – Who would star in your movie?

Chapter 13: Environment...........................109

Quiz 1 – Favorite Animals
Quiz 2 – Spirit Animals
Quiz 3 – Environmental Concerns
Quiz 4 – Apocalypse Blueprint
Quiz 5 – Habitats, Trips, Sightseeing

Quiz 6 – Best Places on Earth

Chapter 14: Fight or Flight........................117

Quiz 1 – What would you do if?
Quiz 2 – Craziest Moments
Quiz 3 – Phobias
Quiz 4 – Public Speaking/Leading
Quiz 5 – If you lived in the old days...
Quiz 6 – Spies and Ninjas

Chapter 15: Random..................................125

Quiz 1 – What would you bring if...?
Quiz 2 – What is your life missing?
Quiz 3 – You won't believe I saw...
Quiz 4 – I can relate most to...
Quiz 5 – Words and Jokes
Quiz 6 – Laughing
Quiz 7 – Books

How to Use This Book

Fuel Creativity

- Creative writing prompts
- Journal / Diary prompts
- Improvisation prompts (ex. Theatre, Dance, Music.)
- Developing fictional characters
- (Books, Movie scripts, Comics)
- Developing personas (Acting Class/ Professional Theater)
- Get the creative juices flowing.

Fuel Curiosity

- Self-Discovery / "Me" time
- Podcast topics
- Ice breakers / Conversation starters
- Quiz Night
- Video topics
- Road trips
- Reminiscing

Chapter 1: Self Expression

Quiz 1 – The Look

Quiz 2 – Interior Design

Quiz 3 – Doodles, Voice, and Songs

Quiz 4 – Influences

The Look

1. What does it mean to have style?

2. What staple articles of clothing are in your closet?

3. What colors look best on you?

4. What colors do you love to wear?

5. If you were a cartoon character and had one signature outfit, what would yours be?

6. What are your favorite hairstyles to wear?

7. What is your favorite piece of jewelry?

8. What is the best accessory to wear daily?

9. With whom would you love to merge closets?

10. What are your go-to shoes?

11. If you had to get rid of everything in your closet, what is the one thing you would keep?

12. What is your favorite season for which to dress?

13. What swimsuit do you feel most confident wearing?

14. Do you have any tattoos, and, if so, why did you get them? (If not, what would you get and why?)

15. Do you have any piercings and, if so, why did you get
    them? (If not, what would you get and why?)

16. Have you ever dyed your hair? If so, what colors and
    why?

17. What is one hairstyle you have contemplated or one
    you would be too afraid to try, and why?

18. What is your favorite physical feature about yourself?

19. What is something about your style others have
    discouraged or insulted?

20. What is something about your style others admire?

Interior Design

1. What is the value of interior design?

2. Describe the highlights of your room?

3. What is something missing from your home, room, or personal space?

4. What are 3 important qualities of your dream home or dream room?

5. What is more important: a comfortable bed or comfortable couch?

6. Whom have you visited that has a fancy home?

7. Whom have you visited that has a comfortable home?

8. What historical period had the strongest architecture and home designs?

9. What DIY projects, if any, have you completed?

10. What is the best home or room-oriented gift you have received?

Doodles, Voice, and Songs

1. What is your go-to paper doodle?

2. Describe the characteristics of your penmanship?

3. How do you hold your writing utensil?

4. What is your favorite writing tool?

5. Name someone who creates interesting page doodles.

6. How do you mark up your paper when taking notes?

7. Do you prefer humming or whistling?

8. What song is always on your mind?

9. Can you name three songs for which you know all the lyrics?

10. Whose singing voice does yours most resemble and why? (Sound quality, not talent.)

11. Can you describe your laughter?

12. Can you describe your crying?

13. How does your voice change when you speak to different individuals?

14. Who can you do a great voice impression of, and why?

15. What accents can you imitate?

16. Do you speak quietly or loudly?

17. If you could have someone else's voice, whose voice would it be and why?

18. Who has the funniest voice you have ever heard and why?

19. Do you know how to project your voice?

Influences

1. Who inspires your style and why?

2. Who (and what) inspired your home and room designs?

3. Who is your role model and why?

4. What is your opinion on cosmetic makeup? Who is someone whose cosmetic make-up (or lack of) inspires you?

5. Name someone whose public speaking style you admire.

6. Name someone whose sense of humor you admire.

7. How persuasive are you? Who is someone you consider persuasive?

8. Who is someone whose online presence inspires you?

9. Who in your immediate family or friend group inspires you?

10. What gives you confidence to be yourself?

Chapter 2: Creativity

Quiz 1 – Experience and Opinion

Quiz 2 – The Arts

Quiz 3 – Creative Process

Quiz 4 – Inventions

Quiz 5 – Creative Problem Solving

Quiz 6 – Creative Hybrids

Experience and Opinion

1. What does it mean to be creative?

2. What does it mean to lack creativity?

3. Is creativity valuable? How would you rate the importance of creativity?

4. Who is the most creative person you know and why?

5. Who is the least creative person you know and why?

6. What animal species do you consider "creative animals?"

7. Have you ever been called creative, if so, why?

8. Who was the first person to call you creative and why?

9. What is the "most creative" project you have completed?

10. What about your everyday life is creative?

11. What about your everyday life is the least creative?

The Arts

1. Name your favorite creative art in which you practice/participate?

2. What is your favorite art to spectate?

3. What do you value more, visual arts or performing arts?

4. Would you rather improve your visual or performing art skills?

5. Do you consider yourself an artist, if so, why?

6. What makes someone an artist?

7. What is your perception of "artist?"

8. Where is the best place to experience visual art?

9. Where is the best place to experience performing art?

10. How do you practice arts daily?

The Creative Process

1. What does it mean to have a creative process, and do you have one?

2. What is the opposite of a creative process?

3. Can you describe the creative process of someone you know or admire?

4. How are you creative in ways you may not realize?

5. What criteria must be met for you to feel successfully creative?

6. How and when is your creative process inappropriate?

7. What is a concept you struggle to understand?

8. How do you process directions and information others share with you?

9. How have others attempted to alter your creative process?

10. How does your creative process stay intact as well as evolve?

Inventions

1. How many inventors have you studied or learned about?

2. What is the role of an inventor in society?

3. Do you have to be innovative to be an inventor?

4. Are you an inventor or capable of inventing?

5. What is a game you or a member of your family invented?

6. What is a food dish you or a member of your family invented?

7. Have you ever plagiarized?

8. What is an invention you highly value and use in your everyday life?

9. Do you think it's possible for one to generate original ideas and thoughts?

10. What do you think will be necessary to usher humanity into the next great era of innovation?

Creative Problem Solving

1. Are you a strong problem solver?

2. Do others consider you a strong problem solver?

3. What are the characteristics of people considered problem solvers?

4. Do you work well when stressed?

5. Are you internally motivated or externally motivated?

6. What is your problem-solving process?

7. Who do you reference when you need help solving problems?

8. Do you enjoy problem-solving?

9. On average, how many problems do you encounter daily?

10. Are problems positive or negative?

11. Do you or others cause your problems?

Creative Hybrids

1. What is the best dinner combo?

2. What is the best dessert combo?

3. What is the best drink combo?

4. What are the best fashion trend combinations?

5. What is the best hybrid animal?

6. What is the best "combination" to experience during the summer?

7. What is the best book-to-movie adaptation?

8. What is the best video game-to-movie adaptation?

9. Who is the best superhero team-up combo?

10. Who is the best hero-villain combination?

Chapter 3: Finances

Quiz 1 – Financial Finesse

Quiz 2 – Rich Mom

Quiz 3 – Poor Mom

Quiz 4 – Hustle and Jive

Quiz 5 – The Art of Money

Quiz 6 – Financial Goals

Financial Finesse

1. How would you describe (the concept of) "finances?"

2. What is the best form of currency?

3. What establishment in existence has the most intriguing currency?

4. Overall, do you prefer coins, dollars, or cards?

5. What is something people in your country frequently purchase?

6. Do school systems and governing bodies properly educate the public on finances?

7. Do you understand the financial climate of your country at this time?

8. Do you manage any investments currently, if so, what are your investments?

9. How do you believe the perception of money and currency has altered during your lifetime?

10. At what age should citizens be allowed to manage their finances?

Rich Mom

1. Do you consider yourself rich?

2. How do you spend most of your money?

3. What's something you would love to purchase at this moment?

4. When was the last time you splurged on yourself?

5. What charity would you like to donate 1 million dollars toward?

6. What is the highest amount of money someone has gifted you?

7. What is something you desired to own as a child, and do you own it now?

8. If money was not an object, what gift would you purchase for a loved one?

9. What critique do you have for someone who is wealthier than you?

Poor Mom

1. Do you consider yourself poor?

2. What is something you regret purchasing?

3. What is the least costly expense in your life?

4. Have you ever been judged for your economic status?

5. Have you ever felt inferior because of your economic status?

6. Have you felt superior to another because of your economic status?

7. What is the worst financial advice you received?

8. What is your worst financial habit?

9. Who or what influences your finances?

10. What is one recurring expense you hate paying and why?

Hustle and Jive

1. What does it mean to hustle?

2. Are you a hustler?

3. What is/ are your hustle(s)?

4. What is a side hustle, and do you have one?

5. Who teaches others to hustle?

6. Who is someone with hustle you admire and why?

7. Who is someone you know that lacks hustle and why?

8. How far are you willing to go to follow your dreams? (Give an example.)

9. What obstacles negatively impact your hustle?

10. What is the opposite of a hustler?

The Art of Money

1. Is budgeting a form of art?

2. Who taught you your current financial skills?

3. If you taught a course on "money" what topics would you teach?

4. What do you know about the origin of money and the individuals responsible for creating and distributing money?

5. Describe the most interesting coin you owned or own?

6. What is your favorite "mock-money" or "play money?"

7. What games can one play that allows the players to practice handling money (or currency?)

8. What environment or setting jeopardizes one's finances and why?

9. What environment improves one's finances and why?

Financial Goals

1. What are your primary financial goals?

2. What is an investment you hope to acquire or purchase in the future?

3. How do you desire to invest in your home or living space?

4. Would you like to invest in a child or animal (in your life) at this time, and why or why not?

5. Would you ever sponsor another person?

6. Do friends and family share financial goals they wish for you? If so, how does that make you feel and behave?

7. What is something you're unable to save money towards now, but will save towards in the future?

8. How do you "give back" to others?

9. How do others "give back" toward you?

Chapter 4: Food Drinks Sleep

Quiz 1 – Foodies

Quiz 2 – Ice Cold Drinks

Quiz 3 – Sleep Preferences

Quiz 4 – Wild Things

Quiz 5 – Kitchen & Cooking Habits

Quiz 6 – Sleep Habits

Foodies

1. Quick! What is your favorite food?

2. What is your favorite (specific) time of day to eat, and why?

3. Do you enjoy breakfast, lunch, or dinner meals most?

4. What is a food you love that you frequently ate as a child?

5. What is a food you hate that you frequently ate as a child?

6. What foods grow in your community?

7. What is your philosophy on diets?

8. What food group do you navigate towards when snacking?

9. What is your go-to snack?

10. What is the best food to share with others?

Ice Cold Drinks

1. Quick! What is your favorite beverage?

2. What beverages did you love growing up?

3. Do you prefer hot drinks or cold drinks?

4. What is your philosophy on ice?

5. What corporation produces the best beverages?

6. On average, how much water do you consume daily?

7. Do you prefer ice cold or room temperature water?

8. How is water sourced in your community/townshhip?

9. Do you consume tap water?

10. Have you ever invented a drink, if so, what drink?

Sleep Preferences

1. What times do you normally sleep?

2. On average how many hours do you sleep during the night?

3. What environmental factors make it difficult for you to sleep?

4. Other than your bedroom, what room or living space makes you easily fall asleep?

5. What sounds help you sleep?

6. Can you sleep with the lights on?

7. Do you use sleep aids to help you sleep?

8. Do you wake up to use the bathroom during the middle of the night or wait until the morning?

9. Do you frequently sleep through the night?

10. Do you frequently dream?

11. Describe the body position in which you sleep.

Wild Things

1. Do you eat other animals?

2. What is the strangest food you have tried?

3. What is the most bizarre food you have seen another person eating?

4. What is the weirdest thing you have seen a different species eating?

5. Have you ever fed wild or stray animals?

6. What animals have diets that disgust you, and what animals have diets that inspire you?

7. Do you eat wildlife from bodies of water?

8. Can you eat bugs?

9. What is your favorite "genre" of food?

10. Who is the best chef/cook you know outside of your family?

Kitchen & Cooking Habits

1. What is one rule about the kitchen by which all members of your household must abide?

2. How often do you use the kitchen, and why?

3. Do you like to clean as you cook, or after you cook?

4. What are your favorite cooking tools and equipment?

5. How would you describe the state and organization of your refrigerator?

6. Do you believe in using microwaves? Why or why not?

7. What is something you do in your kitchen that others might find strange?

8. Who has molded and inspired your relationship with – and use of – your kitchen?

9. Should people be allowed to watch television while they eat, or should they eat in silence/ chat with family members?

10. How often do you wash your hands and wash your produce?

Sleep Habits

1. Are you a morning person, or night person?

2. How do you prefer to wake up? (Do you choose to wake up with an alarm, by a family member, or do you like to sleep in?)

3. On Which side of the bed do you prefer to sleep? (Right or Left? Near a window or on the bed edge?)

4. Do you sleep with a stuffed animal?

5. Do you sleep with pillows? If so, how many and what kinds?

6. Do you like to cuddle? If so, what is your cuddling style?

7. What is your night-care routine?

8. What makes you instantly sleepy?

9. Do you need naps or have time for naps?

10. What time of day is your prime time of day?

Chapter 5: Community and Society

Quiz 1 – Fears and Hopes

Quiz 2 – Politics

Quiz 3 – Economics

Quiz 4 – Education

Quiz 5 – Environment

Fears and Hopes

1. What is your greatest fear about society?

2. What is the most significant public threat to society?

3. Who is the greatest public threat to society?

4. What is your greatest hope for society?

5. Who is your greatest hope for society?

6. Do you believe in conspiracy theories?

7. What is one conspiracy theory you believe?

8. What is one conspiracy theory you think is ridiculous?

9. Who regulates societal trends?

10. Have you ever experienced Déjà vu or the "Mandela Effect?" If so, when?

Politics

1. How are you involved in politics?

2. Are you politically aware?

3. How would you describe the political landscape of your community?

4. How would you describe the political landscape of your home?

5. Have you ever desired to be a politician?

6. How would you alter politics in America?

7. Who is your favorite politician?

8. Who is your least favorite politician?

9. Who is someone in your life who, in your opinion, would make a great politician?

10. What is one law you think should be reformed?

Economics

1. What is your stance on capitalism, communism, and socialism?

2. What are the pros and cons of your country's current economic state?

3. If you could design a financial system, how would it look?

4. What should minimum wage be?

5. Do you think the gap between the rich and the poor is shrinking?

6. What jobs do you think are overpaid?

7. What jobs do you think are underpaid?

8. Should the government step in to subsidize more systems?

9. Should governments be in charge of funding roads and prisons?

10. What is your stance on paying taxes?

Gender Roles

1. What is gender?

2. How many genders exist?

3. What are gender roles?

4. What is the difference between sex and gender?

5. Who taught you about gender roles, and do you continue to uphold those taught beliefs?

6. What is your stance on youth under 18 years of age undergoing sex-change operations?

7. What is your view on preferred pronouns?

8. Do animals have genders?

9. How has gender identity changed over the past ten years?

10. How much of a role does gender play in an individual's character and personality?

Education

1. How important is education?

2. What is your highest level of education, and are you satisfied with your answer?

3. What is your stance on private and public education?

4. Should college be government-funded?

5. How does the education system fail students?

6. How has your formal education affected your current personal life?

7. What is your most fond memory of/at school?

8. On macro and micro levels, how would you change the education system for the better?

9. What is your stance on homeschooling?

10. What are the most critical years in a child's life?

Environment

1. How do you impact the environment daily?

2. What are some things you do that help and hurt the environment?

3. What is the most pressing environmental problem for your community?

4. What is your stance on climate change and global warming?

5. What is your view on human-induced animal extinction?

6. What is your perspective on the meat industry?

7. Do you believe humans should wear fake fur?

8. What quantity of products in your home are derived directly from nature and wildlife?

9. What is your stance on "old industry?"

10. What should be the primary mode of transportation in the future?

Chapter 6: Jobs, Careers, Purpose

Quiz 1 – Dream Jobs

Quiz 2 – Job Stereotypes

Quiz 3 – Overall Opinion

Quiz 4 – Work Readiness

Quiz 5 – Customer Service

Quiz 6 – Vacations

Dream Jobs

1. What is your current dream job, and why?

2. What was/is your first dream job?

3. What is your most supported dream job?

4. What is your least supported dream job?

5. What is the most obnoxious dream job you have ever heard someone claim, and why?

6. What is the most practical dream job you have heard someone claim, and why?

7. How are you now living your dream through work?

8. How are you unfulfilled in the pursuit of your dreams through work?

9. What is the best advice someone has shared with you about dream jobs?

10. What is the best advice you can share with another on dream jobs?

Job Stereotypes

1. What is the most respected profession?

2. What is the least honorable profession?

3. What kinds of jobs do individuals in your family/friend circle gravitate toward, and why?

4. What job is challenging, and why?

5. What jobs are comfortable, and why?

6. What job is scary, and why?

7. What jobs require a great deal of luck?

8. What jobs require great bouts of bravery?

9. What jobs require emotional detachment?

10. What jobs demand great teamwork and the ability to act independently as well?

Overall Opinions

1. What is your opinion on doctors and nurses?

2. What is your opinion on teachers and educators?

3. What is your opinion on Lawyers?

4. What is your opinion on designers?

5. What is your opinion on performers?

6. What is your opinion on chefs and food service workers?

7. What is your opinion on sex workers?

8. What is your opinion on law enforcement?

9. What is your opinion on office workers?

10. What is your opinion on stay-at-home parents?

Work Readiness

1. Are you prepared to be a working citizen? Why or why not?

2. What events in your life have prepared you for the full-time roles you now take on?

3. What characteristics make a great worker?

4. What factors make a poor worker?

5. What are great habits for an employee?

6. What are productive practices for a manager?

7. What are great habits for a business owner?

8. Do you need to train for a job position, or learn while in a job position?

9. How have you been promoted in your work?

10. What encouraged you to start working?

Customer Service

1. What does it mean to have excellent customer service skills?

2. Can you rate your customer service skills from 1-10 (1 being the lowest, 10 being the highest), and why did you choose your rating?

3. How would a stranger rate your customer service skills from 1-10 (1 being the lowest, 10 being the highest), and why?

4. When is a time you have dealt with a challenging customer or client?

5. When is a time you have disrespected a customer or client?

6. Where and how does one learn customer service skills?

7. Who is someone who embodies the perfect customer service agent?

8. What does it say about an individual if they have excellent customer service skills?

9. What does it say about an individual if they have poor customer service skills?

10. What establishment have you attended that has terrific customer service?

11. What establishment have you visited that had horrible customer service?

Vacations

1. Where is your dream vacation destination?

2. Where has been your favorite vacation destination thus far, and why?

3. What is your relationship with travel?

4. Who is your favorite traveling companion, and why?

5. Who would you hate to go on vacation with, and why?

6. What is your favorite mode of transportation for vacations?

7. How much vacation time are you allotted annually, and how content are you with that answer?

8. Have you ever had to travel for work, and if so, how did you feel about that adventure?

9. Do you think everyone should travel outside their country?

10. How do you feel about stay-at-home versus away-from-home vacations?

Chapter 7: The Present of the Past

Quiz 1 – 10 Years Ago

Quiz 2 – School Memories and Field Trips

Quiz 3 – Old Appearances, Looks, Fashion

Quiz 4 – People Who Hurt, Heal, and Humor

Quiz 5 – Parenting and Elder Care

Quiz 6 – Home Remedies and Cures

10 Years Ago

1. How old were you 10 years ago?

2. What was your biggest struggle 10 years ago?

3. Who did you live with 10 years ago?

4. What did you eat 10 years ago?

5. What entertainment did you enjoy 10 years ago?

6. How much money did you own 10 years ago?

7. Who was your greatest enemy, and who was your best friend 10 years ago?

8. What were your biggest goals and dreams 10 years ago?

9. What was always on your mind 10 years ago?

10. What is something you didn't think about 10 years ago that you often think about now?

School Memories and Field Trips

1. What year was your favorite year of school, and why?

2. What year was your least favorite year of school, and why?

3. Who is your favorite teacher and favorite school mate?

4. What was one thing unique about your school experience?

5. What was your favorite field trip as a child?

6. What is your most horrific school memory?

7. What is your funniest school memory?

8. What is your most annoying school memory?

9. When was a time you were rude to a teacher?

10. When was a time you connected with a teacher?

Old Appearances, Looks, Fashion

1. How old were you when you were able to pick out your own clothing?

2. How old were you when you were able to style your own hair?

3. How were you inspired by the fashion of your friends and family?

4. Did you have a lot of hand-me-downs?

5. What was your favorite thing to wear as a child?

6. What was your signature hairstyle?

7. What were some things you were made fun of for wearing? What were somethings you were praised for wearing?

8. How would you best describe your fashion and style in your youth?

9. What was the first fashion rule you learned or heavily enforced?

10. What were some of the "latest trends" during your childhood?

People Who Hurt, Heal, and Humor

1. Who is the person who has made you laugh the most throughout your childhood?

2. Who is the person who made you cry the most throughout your life?

3. Who is the person that made you the angriest throughout your life?

4. Who are the people you made laugh the most throughout your life?

5. Who is the person you made the happiest throughout your life?

6. Who is the person you made the angriest throughout your life?

7. When was a time you had an emotional outburst?

8. When was the last time you had a genuine burst of laughter?

9. When was the last time you cried?

10. When was your first major cry?

Parenting and Elder Care

1. How old are your parents, and how do you feel about their age? How do they feel about their age?

2. Who are your favorite guardians in your life, and why? What do you love about your guardians?

3. If you could pick the parents you were born to, who would you select?

4. How are you most like the adult figures in your life?

5. What is one rule your parents/guardians enforced when growing up, that you currently support.

6. Growing up, what was one rule your parents/ guardians enforced that you do not support?

7. How do you, would you, or will you raise your children
    differently than your parents/guardians?

8. What is your opinion on senior living/nursing homes?

9. What is your overarching view on the elderly?

10. At what age should you be considered an adult, and
    what rights should one receive when one turns that
    age?

Home Remedies and Cures

1. When was a time you were extremely sick?

2. When was a time you were extremely healthy?

3. How often per year are you sick, and how does becoming sick influence your life?

4. What is your remedy and solution for the flu?

5. What is your treatment and solution for a common cold?

6. What are some recipes and food you like to have when you are under the weather?

7. How often do you go to the doctors, and why?

8. How frequently do you pretend to be sick to skip school, work, or special events?

9. When were you the most afraid of a disease or pandemic?

10. What is the secret to health and longevity?

Chapter 8: The Future

Quiz 1 – Predictions

Quiz 2 – Personal Goals

Quiz 3 – Technology

Quiz 4 – Time Travel and Superpowers

Quiz 5 – What Needs to Come Back?

Quiz 6 – Outer Space

Predictions

1. What will the environment look like in the future?

2. What will the economy look like in the future?

3. What will the government look like in the future?

4. How will transportation look in the future?

5. How will technology look in the future?

6. What will war be like in the future?

7. What will families look like in the future?

8. What will race, and nationality look like in the future?

9. What will food look like in the future?

10. What will sleep look like in the future?

Personal Goals

1. What will your life look like in 1 year?

2. What will your life look like in 5 years?

3. What will your life look like in 10 years?

4. What will your life look like in 25 years?

5. What are your hopes for the future of the children in your life?

6. What are your hopes for your current closest friends?

7. What do you hope your health looks like in the future?

8. What do you hope your love life looks like in the future?

9. What questions do you have now that you hope will be answered in the future?

10. What do you hope your spiritual life will look like in the future?

Technology

1. What will kitchen technology look like in the future?

2. What will self-care appliances look like in the future?

3. What is something you want to invent?

4. What is something we need to get rid of in the future?

5. What is something we need in the future?

6. What will children's toys look like in the future?

7. What will technology classes look like in the future?

8. Can you name one modern-day inventor?

9. What is one invention you are looking forward to in the future?

10. How is technology going to change the world in the future?

Time Travel and Superpowers

1. What era would you love to live in for one year?

2. Who is one historical figure you would like to have a conversation with?

3. What is the best and worst time travel-based movie you have seen?

4. Do you believe time travel is real?

5. If we could time travel today what would that process look like and what would the rules be?

6. What is your favorite superpower?

7. What is a skill you have now that could be considered a "superpower?"

8. Where do superpowers come from?

9. Who is worthy of superpowers and how should powers be used?

10. What is one memory you would love to relive?

What Needs to Come Back?

1. What household appliances need to come back, and why?

2. What fashions need to make a comeback, and why?

3. What music needs to come back, and why?

4. What social values need to come back, and why?

5. What laws need to come back, and why?

6. What dating trends need to come back, and why?

7. Which celebrities need to come back, from what era, and why?

8. What commercials need to come back?

9. What movie sequel needs to be created?

10. What historical figure needs to come back?

Outer Space

1. What is your favorite planet?

2. What is your favorite outer space feature and why?

3. Would you ever want to visit the moon?

4. How do you feel about humans exploring outer space?

5. If we could create a planet, how would that planet function?

6. Do you believe in aliens?

7. Do you know any constellations?

8. How many references to the names of planets can you think of in one minute?

9. How long could you live on a spaceship?

10. How much should people pay to travel to outer space?

Chapter 9: Pop Culture

Quiz 1 – Music

Quiz 2 – Movies/TV

Quiz 3 – Games

Quiz 4 – Fashion

Quiz 5 – Stars

Quiz 6 – Dances, Festivals, and Outings

Music

1. What is the first song you ever learned?

2. What is your favorite song now?

3. What are song lyrics that confuse you or you don't understand the words?

4. What kind of music did you grow up around?

5. What is your favorite genre/style of music?

6. What do you value in music?

7. What song is always in your head?

8. What is your favorite holiday song?

9. What type of music do you hate?

10. Can you sing?

Movies/TV

1. What is the first movie you fell in love with?

2. What is the first television show you fell in love with?

3. What is your opinion on kissing scenes in movies?

4. What is your worst movie experience?

5. What are some movies that have made you cry?

6. What is a TV show that you are addicted to?

7. What is your favorite film/TV screening platform?

8. Have you or do you know someone that has been in a movie?

9. What is a TV show you couldn't get into, and why?

10. What is a great TV show or movie someone recommended to you that you would recommend to others?

Games

1. What is your favorite board game?

2. What is your least favorite board game?

3. What is your favorite video game?

4. What is your least favorite video game?

5. What is your favorite cellphone/tablet game?

6. What is your least favorite cellphone/tablet game?

7. What is your favorite gym game?

8. What is your least favorite gym game?

9. What is your favorite outside game?

10. What is your least favorite outside game?

11. What is your favorite party game?

12. What is your least favorite party game?

13. What is your favorite card game?

14. What is your least favorite card game?

15. What is your favorite childhood game?

16. What is your favorite grown up game?

Fashion

1. What is your favorite and least favorite style of shirts?

2. What is your favorite and least favorite style of pants?

3. What is your favorite and least favorite style of dress?

4. What is your favorite and least favorite style of suits?

5. What is your favorite and least favorite style of shoes?

6. What is your favorite and least favorite styles of coats?

7. What is your favorite and least favorite style of swimsuits?

8. What is your favorite and least favorite style of undergarment?

9. What is your favorite and least favorite style of uniforms?

10. What is your favorite and least favorite style of pajamas?

Stars

1. When you read/hear the word "celebrity" who immediately comes to mind?

2. Who do you think is a "handsome" celebrity?

3. Who do you think is a "beautiful" celebrity?

4. Who do you think is a "scandalous" celebrity?

5. What celebrity do you most look like?

6. Who is someone you wish had become more successful in their career?

7. Who is your favorite athlete?

8. Who is your celebrity crush?

9. Who is your favorite internet star?

10. Who is your favorite radio host?

11. Who is your favorite talk show host?

Dances, Festivals, and Outings

1. What was your first music concert?

2. What has been the best live performance you have seen?

3. Have you ever gone to a major festival?

4. What festivals have you gone to throughout your life?

5. Have you ever seen a circus? If so, what is your favorite act?

6. Have you ever been to a convention? If so, which ones?

7. Have you ever been to a professional conference?

8. Have you ever given a public speech or hosted a seminar?

9. What is a festival or public gathering you dream of attending?

10. Who is someone you would love to see perform live?

Chapter 10: Milestones

Quiz 1 – Marriage

Quiz 2 – Birthdays

Quiz 3 – Driving

Quiz 4 – Holidays

Quiz 5 – Transportation

Quiz 6 – Health Consciousness

Marriage

1. Are you married or dating?

2. Do you desire to be married or to be in a committed relationship?

3. Do you believe you need to be legally married to be married in "the eyes of God?"

4. Who is someone you see as having an "ideal" marriage?

5. What is your view on wedding ceremonies?

6. What kind of bridal dresses and grooms suits do you like?

7. Why do people get divorced?

8. Why do people get married?

9. What is a marriage expectation/standard you hope to establish/set up with your significant other?

10. How much should a wedding cost?

11. How long have you personally known a couple to be married?

Birthdays

1. What was your first birthday like?

2. What birthday is the most important birthday?

3. Do you prefer cake, cupcakes, or ice-cream?

4. What birthday was your best birthday?

5. What year was your worst birthday?

6. Did you ever share your birthday with a friend or sibling?

7. What is the most glamorous birthday party you have attended or hosted?

8. What is your opinion of first birthdays?

9. What is the most disappointing birthday party you have attended?

10. What venue is the best to have a birthday party for people your age?

11. What venue is the best to have a child's birthday party?

Driving

1. When was the first time you drove a car?

2. Who taught you how to drive, or who will teach you how to drive?

3. Do you have any driving phobias?

4. Who is the best and worst driver you know?

5. What was your scariest car-related experience?

6. Have you ever been trapped in a car?

7. What is the most terrifying weather condition to drive through?

8. Do you prefer a car with no AC or no heat?

9. What entertainment do you enjoy more when driving CD, radio, or Bluetooth?

10. How do you feel when animals ride in cars?

Holidays

1. Do you celebrate holidays?

2. What is the most overrated holiday?

3. What is the most underrated holiday?

4. What is the most important holiday to spend with family?

5. What is the most important holiday to spend with friends?

6. What holiday should be eliminated and why?

7. What holiday should everyone have off of school and work?

8. Is your birthday on a holiday or a special date?

9. What is your favorite winter holiday memory?

10. What is your worst winter holiday memory?

Transportation

1. What are your immediate thoughts on giant trucks?

2. Have you ever been on an airplane and what are the best and worst parts of the experience?

3. Would you ever ride a motorcycle?

4. When was the last time you rode on a boat?

5. Do you prefer taking a bus or train?

6. Would you ever try driving a monster truck?

7. Can you skateboard or roller-blade?

8. Do you push or ride on shopping carts?

9. What is your opinion on bicycle riding?

10. Should horseback riding be legal?

Health Consciousness

1. What was the most popular diet fad you remember from your childhood?

2. Are you a vegan or vegetarian?

3. What is the most valuable form of exercise?

4. What one food does someone need every day to stay healthy?

5. What is the most harmful drink one can consume?

6. What is your opinion on bulimia and anorexia?

7. What is your opinion on mental health in America today?

8. How often do you go to the doctor per year?

9. Do you know your resting heart rate, average blood sugar level, and cholesterol? Should you know this?

10. Do you have any tips to make your teeth whiter and eyes whiter?

11. What is the scariest tool a physician or dentist uses at a regular checkup exam?

Chapter 11: Spirituality

Quiz 1 – Religious Upbringing

Quiz 2 – Current Beliefs

Quiz 3 – Best Life Experiences

Quiz 4 – Life Rituals

Quiz 5 – Personal Maintenance and Rejuvenation

Quiz 6 – Health Consciousness

Religious Upbringings

1. What was the primary religion or philosophy of your family?

2. What are religious holidays your family observes?

3. What are religious rites of passage your family observes?

4. Who was the most religious person in your childhood?

5. Who is the least religious person in your life from your childhood?

6. What did your upbringing teach you about family and religion?

7. What did your upbringing teach you about marriage and religion?

8. What did your upbringing teach you about sex and religion?

9. What did your upbringing teach you about destiny and religion?

10. What did your upbringing teach you about life and death?

11. What did your upbringing teach you about religion and the apocalypse?

Current Beliefs

1. Do you believe in God?

2. Do you believe religion is good for humanity?

3. Do you believe in prayer or meditation?

4. Do you believe in karma?

5. Should all humans donate and volunteer?

6. Do you believe all people are inherently evil or good?

7. Are all humans inherently selfish?

8. Is money the root of all evil?

9. Is world peace possible?

10. Do you think justice and equality can exist?

Best Life Experiences

1. Best memory with a parent or guardian?

2. Best memory with a sibling or cousin?

3. Best experience with a classmate?

4. Best experience in an elevator?

5. Best experience waiting in line at a store?

6. Best experience at a movie theater?

7. Best experience home alone?

8. Best experience during a snow day (or cancellation of school or work?)

9. Best experience with an animal?

10. Best experience outdoors?

Life Rituals

1. What is the first thing you do in the morning?

2. What is the last thing you do before falling asleep?

3. What do you do before driving or traveling to a new destination?

4. How do you make your bed/sleeping space?

5. Do you routinely meet with any friends or family members weekly?

6. What is your exercise ritual?

7. How do you prepare yourself before performing or presenting in front of a large collection of people?

8. Do you believe in any superstitions?

9. What do you do when you arrive at work or before you prepare for your daily labor?

10. How do you greet certain members of your family?

Personal Maintenance and Rejuvenation

1. Do you have a skincare routine?

2. How often do you care for or maintain your hair, skin, and nails?

3. Do you have a relaxation routine?

4. Do you find meditation or prayer relaxing?

5. What is something that often stresses you out?

6. What is a stress management tool you have learned or value?

7. Do you prefer to give or receive a massage?

8. Have you ever been to a spa? Do you prefer home spas?

9. What does it look like for you to pamper yourself?

10. What tools/resources do you use to induce relaxation?

Life Codes

1. What is a girl code rule you uphold/respect?

2. What is a boy code rule you uphold/respect?

3. What is an unspoken rule you would uphold in your marriage?

4. What is an unspoken rule on friendship?

5. What is an unspoken rule one should follow when dating?

6. What is a code/rule at your place of work?

7. What is a rule that should exist between parent-child relationships?

8. Do parents have the right to look through their children's personal messages or diaries?

9. Do boyfriends or girlfriends have the right to know each other's phone passwords?

10. Can you date your friend's Ex?

11. If you don't like the person someone you love is dating, do you have the right to tell them that?

12. Is it okay to take office supplies from your job?

13. How much food should one eat when sharing a meal with friends?

14. Who should pay the dinner bill when eating out?

Chapter 12: Biopic

Quiz 1 – Life Stats

Quiz 2 – Family History

Quiz 3 – Hobbies

Quiz 4 – Comfort Zone Definers

Quiz 5 – Socializing Styles

Quiz 6 – Who would star in your movie?

Life Stats

1. What does your name mean?

2. How did you get your name or fun nickname?

3. How old are you?

4. When is your birthday, and what is your zodiac sign and birthstone?

5. Who are your main guardians?

6. How many siblings do you have?

7. Where do you live?

8. Where is your citizenship?

9. What is your profession or primary job?

10. Who are you?

Family History

1. The most impressive profession in your family?

2. The most unique profession in your family?

3. What is the most amount of money/assets your family has owned?

4. Does anyone in your family own a business or wish to own a business?

5. How far back can you trace your family tree?

6. Your ancestors are from which countries?

7. A disease that runs in your family is what?

8. What is a talent most members of your family have?

9. Describe your family dynamic in 3 words?

10. If your family had a TV show what kind of show would it be and who would be the stars?

Hobbies

1. Favorite craft to make?

2. Favorite sport to play?

3. What clubs would you join if you were in school?

4. Favorite thing to collect?

5. What could you talk for hours about?

6. I should volunteer with...

7. Do you enjoy cooking?

8. Do you enjoy being outdoors?

9. Do you enjoy debating and arguments?

10. Do you enjoy "me time?"

Comfort Zone Definers

1. When are you physically uncomfortable?

2. When are you the most physically comfortable?

3. When are you the most socially uncomfortable?

4. When are you the most socially comfortable?

5. What is the bravest thing you have done in your life?

6. Do you consider yourself more fearless, or anxious?

7. What have others taught you about "comfort zones."

8. What do you think about adrenaline junkies and thrill-seekers?

9. Do you ever feel peer pressure to face your fears, and is this good or bad?

10. How do you challenge others to face their fears?

Socializing Styles

1. How do you socialize with your immediate family?

2. How do you socialize with your best friends?

3. How do you socialize with religious leaders?

4. How do you socialize with senior citizens?

5. How do you socialize with your fitness coach?

6. How do you socialize with classmates?

7. How do you socialize with cashiers?

8. How do you socialize with doctors?

9. How do you socialize with those you are sexually attracted to?

10. How do you socialize with people via email?

11. How do you socialize with people through text messages?

12. How do you socialize when leaving comments on social media platforms?

Who would star in your movie?

1. Who would play "you" in a movie?

2. Who would play your romantic lead?

3. Who would play a child in your life?

4. Who would play your antagonist?

5. Who would play your worst boss or favorite employee?

6. Who would play your best friend?

7. Who would play your parents/guardians?

8. Who would play your prominent local government official or church leader?

9. Who would play younger you and older you?

10. Who would play your siblings?

Chapter 13: Environment

Quiz 1 – Favorite Animals

Quiz 2 – Spirit Animals

Quiz 3 – Environmental Concerns

Quiz 4 – Apocalypse Blueprint

Quiz 5 – Habitats, Trips, Sightseeing

Quiz 6 – Best Places on Earth

Favorite Animals

1. What is your favorite safari animal?

2. What is your favorite rain forest animal?

3. What is your favorite nocturnal animal?

4. What is your favorite beach animal?

5. What is your favorite lake animal?

6. What is your favorite local animal?

7. What/who is your favorite zoo animal?

8. What is your favorite domesticated animal?

9. What is your favorite Arctic animal?

10. What is your favorite prairie/grassland animal?

Spirit Animals

1. What is your spirit animal?

2. What animal do you sleep like?

3. What animal diet could you live by?

4. What animal mating/dating/pairing life resembles your own?

5. What animal reflects your parenting style?

6. What animal reflects your work ethic?

7. According to the Chinese Zodiac classification, you were born in the year of the...?

8. What animal do you most resemble?

9. What animal do you wish was your spirit animal?

10. To what extent do you believe in spirit animals?

Environmental Concerns

1. Do you believe in global warming?

2. What are your thoughts on deforestation?

3. Should all people use solar power?

4. What is your view on electric cars?

5. What is an animal on the brink of extinction?

6. What is the greatest, present day, water-related crisis?

7. How often do you litter?

8. Should plastic be legal?

9. What can we do as individuals to keep our planet healthy?

10. Should all people become vegetarians to help the environment?

11. What impact would dramatic regulation on gas, water, and pollution have on the working class?

Apocalypse Blueprint

1. How will the world end?

2. Where will you go to survive the apocalypse?

3. Who will you take with you when the apocalypse is upon us?

4. Do you believe in any prophecies about the end of the world?

5. How will you find water during the apocalypse?

6. What will you eat during the apocalypse?

7. What is in your survival kit?

8. What is your family's current natural disaster plan?

9. Do you or anyone you know have a doomsday vault/ food supply?

10. Do you know your country's current plan if the apocalypse were to occur today?

Habitats, Trips, Sight Seeing

1. What terrain would you like to live in if you didn't live where you currently live?

2. Where in your community do people go to learn about nature?

3. Where do the people in your community go hunting?

4. Where do the people in your community go for shopping sprees?

5. Where do people in your community go to exercise outdoors?

6. What is a common tourist spot in your community?

7. What is a hidden gem tourist should visit in your community?

8. What is a popular camping ground in your community?

9. Where is a teen hangout spot in your community?

10. Where is a senior citizen hangout in your community?

Best Places on Earth

1. Where is the most beautiful garden you have seen?

2. Where is the most beautiful body of water you have seen?

3. Where are the most beautiful displays of artwork you have seen?

4. Where is the most beautiful home you have ever seen?

5. Where are the most beautiful creatures you have ever seen?

6. Where is the most beautiful bathroom you have ever seen?

7. Where is the most beautiful dessert you have seen?

8. Where is the most beautiful collection of people you have seen?

9. Where is the most beautiful collection of one item you have seen?

10. Where is the most beautiful human connection you have made?

Chapter 14: Fight or Flight

Quiz 1 – What would you do if?

Quiz 2 – Craziest Moments

Quiz 3 – Phobias

Quiz 4 – Public Speaking/Leading

Quiz 5 – If you lived in the old days...

Quiz 6 – Spies and Ninjas

What would you do if...?

1. A mountain lion ran towards you?

2. You ripped your pants right now?

3. The power went out for 3 days?

4. Your car died in the middle of the road?

5. You found a roach or rat in your tub?

6. You saw someone was being robbed?

7. You found $100 on the ground?

8. The toilet flooded the bathroom?

9. You lost your job, or were kicked out of school/ the house?

10. "Future you" time-traveled to "present-day you" and told you to stay home tomorrow at all cost?

Craziest Moments

1. When was the time you were most afraid for your life?

2. When is a time you were most afraid to speak to someone?

3. When is a time you were the angriest you had ever been in your life?

4. When was the time you were the "hangriest" (hungry & angry) in your life?

5. When is the time you were the saddest in your life?

6. When was the last time you threw a temper tantrum?

7. When was someone most afraid of you?

8. When did you make someone extremely sad?

9. When was the last time you intimidated someone?

10. When was the last time you hated someone at first, but they ended up being a close friend?

Phobias

1. What animal are you most afraid of?

2. Are you afraid to burp or fart in public?

3. An article of clothing you could never wear in public?

4. Are you afraid of heights?

5. Are you afraid of the dark?

6. Are you afraid of paranormal activity?

7. What foods are you afraid to consume?

8. Are you afraid of any authoritative figures in your life?

9. Are you afraid of any water-related activities such as boats or swimming?

10. Are you afraid of any movies?

11. Are you afraid of roller coasters?

12. Do you experience social anxiety?

13. How have you overcome any childhood fears?

Public Speaking/ Leading

1. In what ways are you a leader?

2. What is your style of leadership?

3. Who is an inspiring leader in your life?

4. Are you bossy or controlling? In general, are leaders bossy and controlling?

5. Do you believe in alpha males and alpha females? If so, are you an alpha or beta?

6. Are you a natural performer? Why or why not?

7. How do you overcome stage fright?

8. When was the last time you made a public announcement or speech?

9. What is the best leadership advice you've received?

10. Would you prefer to speak in front of a large crowd or a smaller, more intimate crowd?

If you lived in the old days...

1. How would you survive ancient Egypt?

2. How would you survive the Victorian era?

3. How would or did you survive the 1990s?

4. How would you survive the Stone Age?

5. How would you survive the Edo period?

6. How would you survive the Mayan Classic period?

7. How would you survive the Elizabethan Era?

8. How would you survive the great depression?

9. How would you survive the Golden Age of India?

10. How will you survive the years to come?

Spies and Ninjas

1. Would you ever want to serve as a law enforcement agent?

2. Do you know self-defense?

3. Could you pass a lie detector test?

4. Do you value stealth or strength?

5. Have you ever been in a physical fight and how did it end?

6. Have you ever seen people physically fighting?

7. What is your weapon of choice?

8. How are you a detective in your everyday life?

9. Are you a good cop, or a bad cop?

10. Who in your life would you hire to act as a spy for a mission?

Chapter 15: Random

Quiz 1 – What would you bring if...?

Quiz 2 – What is your life missing?

Quiz 3 – You won't believe I saw...

Quiz 4 – I can relate most to...

Quiz 5 – Words and Jokes

Quiz 6 – Laughing

Quiz 7 – Books

What would you bring if...?

1. You were invited to a celebrity gala?

2. You won a 3-day trip to Las Vegas?

3. You had to be locked in the library overnight?

4. You had to enter a fighting tournament – no rules.

5. You were going on a road trip?

6. You had to live as a house nanny for 1 year?

7. You went to live in a dormitory in japan?

8. You were going to the moon?

9. You knew you were going to Antarctica for the night?

10. You had to go camping in your backyard?

What is your life missing?

1. What is something that you lost as a child?

2. What is something you lent to a friend that was never returned?

3. What is something you think someone stole from you?

4. Have you ever stolen anything from another person or a store?

5. Who is someone you miss in your life?

6. What is something you can no longer eat due to dietary restrictions that you wish you could eat?

7. What are some products you wish you owned to complete your home?

8. What are some products you wish you owned to enhance your primary mode of transportation?

9. What is a milestone life experience you missed out on?

10. What is something that has been removed or taken away from you?

You won't believe what I saw...

1. What is the craziest occurrence you witnessed at school?

2. What was the most outrageous occurrence you witnessed at church or a religious ceremony?

3. What is the scariest thing you witnessed in public?

4. What is the scariest occurrence you witnessed while driving on the road?

5. What is the strangest thing you witnessed in summer?

6. What is the strangest occurrence you witnessed in winter?

7. What is the strangest thing you witnessed while with
    total strangers?

8. What is the weirdest thing you witnessed while sick or
    injured?

9. What is the weirdest thing you witnessed in your
    dream?

10. What is the strangest thing someone has witnessed
    you doing?

I can relate most to...

1. What video game character can you relate to, and why?

2. What CD best describes your life?

3. What movie or show protagonist do you most relate to?

4. Who is a cartoon character you identify with?

5. What celebrity do you most parallel?

6. Who is your doppelganger?

7. Who is someone you know that is most like you but is not a relative?

8. Who is someone that claims you are like family to them?

9. Are you more like your mother or father?

Words and Jokes

1. The saddest word in English?

2. The funniest word in English?

3. The most provocative English word?

4. The sweetest word in English?

5. The best pick-up line you have heard?

6. The joke you can never forget from your childhood?

7. The best knock-knock joke ever?

8. What mnemonic devices can you remember?

9. What is a joke you made up yourself?

Laughing

1. What is the funniest face you can make?

2. What is a hilarious sound?

3. What is the best joke you know?

4. What is the worst joke you know?

5. What is the funniest scene in a movie?

6. What is the funniest song you can think of?

7. Who is the funniest comedian?

8. Who is the funniest person in your life? Who do you make laugh the most in your life?

9. What is the funniest thing you have ever done?

10. Do you believe some people lack a sense of humor?

11. What is the most disturbing thing that made you laugh?

12. What is the difference between funny and silly?

13. How would you describe your sense of humor?

14. What is something others find funny that you do not find funny?

15. When did you have your greatest laugh?

16. Have you ever fake laughed, and why?

17. What is your fake laugh?

18. Who do you know whose laughter makes you laugh?

19. How do you make babies laugh?

20. When has an animal made you laugh?

Books

1. The best children's book?

2. The best scary book?

3. Best book-to-movie adaptation?

4. The worst book-to-movie adaptation?

5. What are books you remember reading with classmates?

6. A book you have researched or done a project about?

7. The Best graphic novel?

8. Best romance novel?

9. Best fantasy novel?

10. Most disappointing book sequel?

11. What is your go-to magazine?

12. What is a book you would never read that everyone loves?

13. A book you are eager to own?